MUSEUM OF ADIRONDACKS

Craig and Alice Gilborn

Craig Gilborn has been director of the Adirondack Museum, Blue Mountain Lake, New York, since 1972. Alice Gilborn is associate editor.

Principal photography is by Karen Halverson, Peter and Rosine Lemon, and Erik Borg.

Copyright © 1984 by the Adirondack Museum
International Standard Book Number 0-910020-36-1
Designed by Peter and Rosine Lemon, Long Lake, New York
Typography by Partners Composition, Utica, New York
Printed by Brodock Press, Inc., Utica, New York

Published by the Adirondack Museum of the Adirondack Historical Association

CONTENTS

THE LAND AND ITS PEOPLE

Alvah Dunning, Adirondack guide

Preceding page:
Samuel Colman, *AuSable River, Adirondacks*

The Adirondacks is a place where nature and not humanity is the measure of things. Although man's incursions are visible, most of the region remains the same today as when the Indians first entered this land of mountain rimmed lakes, tumbling streams and dark forests. The Adirondacks are rich in natural beauty, but they yield little else to the men and women who call them their home. A frugal economy, solitude, and sparsity of human services have molded these residents, some of them third and fourth generation, as surely as the long, cold winters have shaped the tough mountain spruce. This short book is an introduction to the Adirondacks—its land, people and history—as highlighted in the exhibits and collections at the Adirondack Museum in Blue Mountain Lake, New York.

The Adirondacks may be compared with an inland island. *An Inland* *Island* Indeed, this is how the region appears in satellite photographs: forest cover indicated by gray, with a vast network of lakes and streams in jet black, and the whole surrounded by a lighter colored slope of soil and glacial sand descending to the St. Lawrence and Mohawk Rivers on the north and south to Lakes Champlain and Ontario on the east and west. On this outer belt are found farms, many of them dairies, as well as small cities such as Glens Falls, Plattsburgh, Malone, Utica and Herkimer. These communities have served as marketplaces for nearby Adirondack districts, receiving products of the forest and returning cash in the form of employment and taxes. Much shopping, banking and medical attention take Adirondackers to these outlying towns, even though the travel each way may require as much as three hours driving time.

Mountains and rock underlying the cover of forest and lakes *Mountain* give the Adirondacks their distinctive profile; the territory, at least *Profile* for the eastern U.S., is large in extent, embracing six million acres, or an area somewhat larger than the State of Massachusetts. Elevations range from one hundred feet on Lake Champlain to the "High Peaks" district south of Lake Placid where about forty summits exceed sea level by four thousand feet or more. One of these is Mt. Marcy, which at 5,344 feet is the highest point in the state and a traditional challenge to hikers. Few are the Adirondack towns that cannot claim at least one mountain within easy view,

South of St. Huberts by Eliot Porter

8

Aerial view of village of Long Lake

a landmark from which season and weather may be gauged at a knowing glance. Residents of Blue Mountain Lake are luckier than most—they have a mountain in their back yard and a lake at their front door.

Flora and Fauna
Roughly circular in outline, the region contains 2,300 lakes and ponds and 1,200 miles of rivers fed by over 30,000 miles of brooks and streams and 40,000 wetland swamps, bogs and marshes. Nurtured by this brew of water, soil and sand are a diversity of flora and fauna—thirty species of trees and fifty of mammals native to the region. On this inland island each variety of life occupies a niche; one can find, for example, Lapland rosebay in alpine zones and the Lincoln sparrow in lowland bogs and spruce swamps.

Seasons
Just as climate and seasons command the trees, plants and wildlife, so also do they shape the activities, corresponding to the cycles of nature, of year-round residents. Summer is the most hectic season, spring and early fall are times of concentrated preparation for the months ahead, and winter, the longest and harshest period, keeps men and women close to home and personal tasks.

Dominance of Nature
The dominance of nature in the Adirondacks must be understood to appreciate the region's history and its people. Nature can never be muzzled in the Adirondacks; it arbitrarily freezes water pipes, flattens trees and starves the weak, just as it bears the song of the returning warbler in May. It is not easy for man to thrive here. The population, numbering about 120,000 and scattered throughout, is not much greater today than it was seventy years ago. Some towns, including Blue Mountain Lake where the Adirondack Museum is located, have fewer permanent and seasonal residents today than they did at the turn of the century.

Howard and John Seaman of Long Lake, 1977

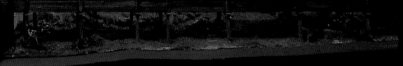

MAKING A LIVING

Decking logs, skidding diorama

While most Americans today have become accustomed to year-round employment at one job, Adirondack residents still need to support themselves at two or three jobs. The seasonal pattern of work tests the Adirondack native's independence and ability to "make do," the results of adaptation to a region where daily life is dictated by nature rather than society.

The Adirondacker has been traditionally a jack-of-all-trades, better at some tasks than others. It is risky to generalize, but the majority of men in the Adirondacks before 1900 probably engaged in at least three of the following in the course of a year or two: farming, logging, trapping, guiding, carpentry and caretaking of private camps and preserves. Except for resort occupations, the skills demanded of the native had their nearest counterpart in New England family life of the Colonial era.

Farming in the Adirondacks was mainly subsistence farming, ***Farmer*** supplying local rather than regional or national markets. The kitchen garden, a family effort, produced food for the home, the hotel, the logging or mining camp. Fresh vegetables graced the table in summer while others were stored in the root cellar for winter consumption. Potatoes, squash, corn and beans were staples, fast-growing and sufficiently hardy to survive late frosts in June and early ones in September. Open fields on the outskirts of towns like Indian Lake and Long Lake are evidence that horses and cows were once pastured there. Old-timers recall seeing distant mountains and lakes where none can be seen now; many fields have reverted to woodland. Field crops—oats, buckwheat, wheat, rye, corn and barley—were grown for flour, meal and feed. Hay was harvested for a farmer's own livestock and as a supplemental crop for logging operations. Chickens, pigs and sheep were raised, as were apples in small orchards. Wild berries—blueberries, blackberries and raspberries—were plentiful for those who knew where to find them. And of course the Adirondacks yielded its own larder, usually abundant, of fish, deer, honey and maple sugar.

Cash, always essential for purchases at the store, was earned by guiding, carpentry and logging. This meant absences from home by the men of the family. A guide during the decade 1885– ***Guide*** 95 could expect to make $2.50 to $3.00, plus expenses, for each day worked in the service of one or two sportsmen. The guide

furnished boat and camp utensils, rowed and carried the boat, and performed necessary camp work, including the preparation of food. As a carpenter or laborer, the Adirondacker might move to the construction site for a hotel or camp as much as fifty miles or so from home, living at the project, or in a boarding house, from spring to autumn.

Logger   It was as logger that the native found his most reliable source of employment. Beginning in Colonial times with the cutting of giant white pine in the Champlain Valley for masts for the British navy, and continuing from the era of floating logs down rivers to our own time when logs are transported by trucks, the wood products industry has employed thousands of residents and given rise to the region's most colorful tales and songs. Logging was seasonal—fall, winter and spring—and encompassed a hierarchy of trades, such as lumberjack, blacksmith, cook, stablehand and so on. A logging camp was cemented by team effort and months of sunup to sundown labor, often hazardous to body and limb. Lumberjacks had healthy appetites. At Blue Mountain Lake forty men were known to have eaten, at one sitting, 400 eggs, three whole hams and innumerable loaves of bread. When they got to town after weeks of isolation in their remote camps, loggers could behave riotously.

Trapping and bounty hunting were sources of income for some **_Trapper_** Adirondackers. The pelts of mink, muskrat and other fur bearing mammals were sold in the spring to buyers from the city. The state, by paying a bounty on the wolf, lynx and panther, hastened the extirpation of these species by about 1910. Overtrapped, the beaver had all but disappeared by the 1890's. Improved management restored some species, including the beaver, to the Adirondacks, and trapping remains a partial source of support for a small number of residents who have the stamina to check their miles of trap lines in the deep of winter.

If any occupation was a test of a person's skills and resource- **_Caretaker_** fulness, it was likely to be that of the caretaker and his wife. Camp maintenance and operation were their responsibilities, no small job when the camp might consist, as did some in the Raquette Lake area, of a dozen cottages and service buildings, a farm enclave with barns and stables, miles of roads, hundreds of acres of forest, and a staff of two to thirty to be fed and supervised. Many duties fell to the wife, who had to be a good cook and manager of the domestic staff, particularly when the owner and guests were in residence. At larger camps like Pine Knot, Uncas and Sagamore, the couple occupied a cottage provided by their employer on the property. Only a few caretakers live at camps today; the majority make periodic visits to a few properties in their charge, checking locks, making minor repairs and opening the camp in summer and closing it in the fall.

Few towns in the Adirondacks lacked a hotel. Blue Mountain **_Summer_** Lake in 1890 had six with accommodations for between a dozen **_Jobs_** and, at the Prospect House, 500 guests. Residents found summer employment in these hotels and in related businesses, such as stage and steamboat lines, which sprang up to serve the surge of visitors each summer. Among employees hired from outside the Adirondacks were young men and women eager to earn money for college; some of these married and settled down in the region.

Another industry that drew people into the Adirondacks was

17

Mining Building

Miners the mining and mineral industry. Usually involving iron extraction and mostly concentrated in the eastern part of the Adirondacks, mining imparted a special character or flavor to many Adirondack communities. Several, such as Mineville, Ironville and Lyon Mountain, were exclusively mining communities. The village and ironworks at MacIntyre (re-named Tahawus), perhaps the most romantic, if ill-fated venture, operated from 1832 to 1856 in the heart of the Adirondack wilderness. Up to one hundred people labored in the isolated village, which had a school, church, bank, store, farm, lumber mill, with cottages for families and a dormitory for unmarried men. Little remains standing today—a clapboard house called the McNaughton Cottage and the giant blast furnace of hewn stone, brick and iron which was erected in 1854.

Mining in the Adirondacks has not been fully appreciated, probably because mining was a local activity and thought to be inimical to the Adirondack environment. However, there were at least three hundred mining or processing sites in the larger Adirondack region, with 75 per cent of them active between 1850 and 1900. Today only a few of these mines are operating. Garnet

Log jam diorama

has been extracted and milled in North River and vicinity for about 100 years, and titanium-bearing ore is mined near the site of the old MacIntyre village. Other minerals which are currently mined are wollastonite, talc and zinc.

Ice harvesting was a major Adirondack industry. Used princi- *Ice* pally for refrigeration, blocks of ice weighing 200 to 250 pounds *Harvest* were cut on lakes and ponds in late January and February when the ice normally is between twenty and thirty inches thick. Ice for local consumption, at hotels and private camps, was stored in ice houses with sawdust laid between the layers for insulation. Large quantities were shipped by railroad to New York and other cities. In 1906, the Raquette Lake Transportation Company con-

Blue Mountain Lake House by Seneca Ray Stoddard

tracted to sell 20,000 tons to the New York Central Railroad, and within a few years more than 50,000 tons were being shipped by rail from Raquette Lake. Despite machines for cutting the ice and conveying it, hard labor and prolonged exposure to the cold were required of the teams of men and older boys who were hired to perform the seasonal harvest of ice.

Gas and electric refrigeration steadily reduced the demand for ice into the 1950's, so that ice cutting is a rare occurrence today. Ice was cut on Raquette Lake in 1982, but the owner of the ice house, which supplies the ice to summer campers with portable coolers, speculated that it might be the last harvest. This would end a winter tradition more than a century old—an inevitable break by an Adirondack community with its past.

Sugaring Off　　Maple sugar sheds, most of them abandoned and derelict, testify to yet another Adirondack activity, the production of maple syrup for home consumption and sale to summer visitors. The tapping of sugar maples and boiling of sap occurred simultaneously, generally between mid-February and mid-March, depending on seasonal conditions. It took about forty gallons of sap, collected from buckets once or twice daily, to produce one gallon of syrup. Keeping up with the run kept family and friends busy from dawn until well after dark, hauling sap in a tub on a horsedrawn sleigh and boiling it down in large iron pans over a fire that required plenty of wood and constant attention.

Commercial production was more common outside than inside the Adirondacks; two exceptions, early this century, were the Horseshoe Forestry Company at Sabattis and the Emporium Forestry Company at Conifer. The Sabattis operation utilized 60,000 buckets and kept five sugar houses busy 24 hours a day. Always somewhat recreational, sugaring is more so today, at least in the Adirondacks; a few old timers, especially in the less rugged territory around Jay and AuSable Forks, still produce quantities of syrup and sugar candy for the summer trade.

A job here and another there does not mean a living wage; at some point spirit and ingenuity are no longer adequate, especially now that the state dictates what a person can and cannot do, namely catch fish or shoot a deer when the cupboard is bare. If the Adirondacker earns a wage for twenty weeks, then he or she is qualified to receive unemployment checks for a somewhat longer period of time. Since tourism is the region's biggest industry, employment soars in July and August but drops like a stone between Labor Day and the end of hunting season in December. And many residents, in what is almost a ritual, return once again to the unemployment line. Unemployment in Hamilton County was 16.6 percent of the workforce in 1973, almost three times the rate for the state as a whole.

Motorized ice saw

21

Museum campus from rustic summerhouse

Sportsman's ideal retreat

Indians have hunted in the Adirondacks for hundreds of years, and as early as the eighteenth century, trappers, guides and a few hardy homesteaders chose to live here. But it was not until the second half of the nineteenth century that improved access began to accelerate settlement. Getting people in and out of the Adirondacks has been the region's salvation and its curse. The mountainous terrain and long winters caused severe transportation problems and retarded the growth of industry and commerce. The ironworks at MacIntyre was an example. Carting pig iron over the wilderness road to the town of Crown Point on Lake Champlain, forty miles to the east, proved so costly and uncertain that it became one of the reasons for the company's closing in 1856. Conversely, the preservation of scenic beauty for which the region is famous is due in large part to the Adirondacks' inability to afford the same ease of access that transformed New York State into a commercial and industrial giant—warts and all—during the nineteenth century.

Today's traveller thinks only of the road, but his predecessor in the last century moved through the Adirondacks both by land and water. Most important to early travel were water routes, chiefly those that followed the north-south corridor of Lakes George and Champlain; and, in the Adirondack heartland, the chain of lakes that extended diagonally from about Old Forge in the southeast to the Saranac Lakes in the northeast. Trappers and guides, like the Indians before them, traversed the roadless wilds by carrying canoes and guideboats from one lake to its neighbor, along "carries" (called "portages" in French Canada) seldom more than a mile or two long. Large enough for a guide, his client and their equipment, the guideboat was easily carried on the guide's shoulders on land. Indigenous to the Adirondacks, it reflected a specific adaptation to the environment.

Canoe and Guideboat

By 1870, steamboat and stagecoach lines, stimulated by growing hordes of tourists, were augmenting the earlier, primitive mode of travel. In 1892 the first trans-Adirondack railroad opened up the interior between Herkimer and Malone. Even so, vast tracts remained isolated and were more conveniently reached by water than by land. The local importance of the guideboat can be imagined by an incident that occurred one dark night in 1882, when the steamboat *Buttercup* was scuttled and sent to the bottom of Long Lake. Rumor held that the deed had been done by a guide

Stage

who resented the competition for carrying travellers on the lake.
Getting to the Adirondacks was not easy. The traveller from New
York City reached Albany by steamboat or rail and continued from
there by train to a station on the outer fringes of the Adirondack
uplands. Three such stops were at Luzerne, Herkimer and West-
port. A horse-drawn stagecoach, buggy or wagon carried him the
rest of the way, though the final leg often required transfer to a
steamboat, or perhaps even a second steamboat. The wretched
conditions of the roads in the Adirondacks made the last link the
worst in the traveller's journey; the 1-1/2 mile hill near North River
was so long and steep that hapless passengers occasionally were
asked by the driver to get out and trudge up or help push the
stage. In 1880 the trip from Manhattan to Blue Mountain Lake took
26 hours to complete, exclusive of layovers.

Railroad   The railroad, harbinger of economic expansion nearly every-
where else, did not transform the Adirondacks as expected by
advocates of its introduction to the region. Investors fancied a
future in which the Adirondacks would become both a resource
plantation and a vacation resort, supplying logs to lumber and

pulp mills on the periphery and drawing tourists and small property owners to its lakes and small communities on the inside. The combination of terrain, climate and cost thwarted these dreams. By 1871, the Adirondack Railroad took passengers and freight as far as North Creek, but cash and state subsidies needed to extend the line another 125 miles to Ogdensburg were never forthcoming.

The first railroad to cross the Adirondacks, from Herkimer in the south to Malone in the north, was built in 1891–92 by Dr. William Seward Webb, who sold it to the New York Central Railroad soon after. Tourists by the thousands and logs in the hundreds of thousands travelled on this and the spur lines reaching Adirondack towns like Lake Placid and Chateaugay from major points

teamboat at Duryea's

outside the region. In 1915, the train traveller could leave New York City at 7:10 P.M. and wake up in Raquette Lake at 7:00 A.M. the next day.

Catching the train was a memorable experience. One who did it often, Harold K. Hochschild, recalled arriving at the Sabattis station in the dark of night:

Inside the station, the station-master, who had retired some hours earlier, had left two railroad oil lanterns for us, one red and one white. Sometimes he'd left them lit; if not, we put a match to the wicks and waited for the sound of the locomotive whistle approaching from the north and finally for the reflected glare of the headlight before the locomotive itself appeared. Then we swung our lanterns and the train thundered to a halt at this tiny station in the wilderness.

Adirondack station master diorama

Dining and sleeping compartments, *Orienta*

Mr. Hochschild, who was chiefly responsible for the founding of the Adirondack Museum, began coming to the Adirondacks as a boy shortly after the turn of the century.

Automobile   The automobile in the Adirondacks undermined the railroad and many established resort hotels. Introduced about 1905, the motorcar created a clamor for more and improved roads. Seneca Ray Stoddard, who published his first guidebook to the Adirondacks in 1873, noted the impact of the automobile in his touring guide for car owners in 1915: "Changes? Wild grass grows on the old routes. ... It is truly a new Adirondacks, a wilderness traversed by magnificent state highways, forming a network of roads as fine as the boulevards of our cities." Families camped at campsites or roadside motels; freed of timetables, they moved from place to place at whim. The sedate vacation at a favorite hotel gradually vanished along with the horse-drawn buggy, the steamboat and ultimately the railroad itself.

Maxwell automobile and early gas station

Bardo family blacksmith shop, 1885–1952

The gasoline shortage and the upcoming Winter Olympics held in Lake Placid in 1980 spurred an attempt to reopen the railroad line between Utica and Lake Placid. Subsidies from the state and Federal governments enabled passenger trains to operate for a brief period during and after the Olympics, but service was slow due to antiquated equipment and a road bed vulnerable to drifting snow and spring washouts. In 1981 the company declared itself bankrupt, and the state began looking for a buyer of miles of steel rails. The car remains king of travel in the Adirondacks, continuing to impress its own reality ever more deeply on the region, to the virtual exclusion of every other mode of travel and, indeed, of life. Modern trailers and vans of today have taken the suburban comforts of the American family's home—kitchen, bathroom and television—to the shores of lakes that were once accessible only to the guide and his canoe or guideboat.

OUTDOOR RECREATION

Hermit's shanty, Noah John Rondeau

The Adirondacks' oldest recreational activity is the hunt. Traditionally this meant stalking the woods for the white-tailed deer or angling in lakes or streams for trout, though other game, such as the moose, which had disappeared from the region by the 1880's, were also hunted.

The perennial trip to the Adirondacks with rod and gun seemed to city-bred men and a few women to be a necessary remedy to the debilitating effects of office and parlor, as prescribed by this passage from *Scribner's Magazine* in 1888:

> *Out of the woods we came, and to the woods we must return, at frequent intervals, if we would redeem ourselves from the vanities of civilization.*

Even a vigilant guide at one's side and an ample supply of beans and pork in the pack did not diminish the survival aspects of the hunt. So, too, there were rewards of a spiritual sort, as illustrated by an evocation of 1882:

> *The campfire burns brightly ... The waters croon a drowsing lullaby, the stars o'erhead keep watch and ward. Healing and strength come with every in-breathing of this pine-blest air. This is re-creation.*

Indians

Surface discoveries of Indian implements—stone and pottery fragments—indicate that Indians foraged in the Adirondacks perhaps as long ago as 1,800 years before the arrival of Europeans. Archaeologists believe that the migration was seasonal—the Indians arriving in warm months and retreating to their home grounds in the lowlands before winter. If true, this seasonal migration is the oldest continuing pattern of human behavior in the Adirondacks. Possibly the Indians came not merely to seek food for survival but to escape from the warmer temperatures of outlying valleys.

Sir William Johnson's Hideaway

The Adirondacks as a playground for relaxation and sport dates from the late Colonial period. In 1770, Sir William Johnson, an agent of the British Crown to the Indians, erected a cottage and what a later writer termed a "little log tenement" on land now submerged under the Sacandaga Reservoir. Called Mount Joy, this rustic retreat was fifteen miles from Johnson's fine Georgian home in Johnstown to the south. More typical of early settlement was the log cabin built about 1800 by Jock Wright, a trapper who was a veteran of the Battle of Bunker Hill, on Jock's Lake. A hotel was later built on the site.

43

Starting about 1825, small parties of men would enter the Adirondacks by wagon at any of six or so gateway towns, and then move through a locale under the watchful eye of what became the legendary Adirondack guide, a man familiar with outdoor living and a particular territory usually near home. Early on, year-round residents found footsore sportsmen at the door begging for food and a place to spend the night. These havens, strategically placed, occasionally evolved into hotels.

Early Travel Wilderness trips entailed discomforts. Looking back to the 1850's, W. E. Wolcott reminisced:

> *Those were the days of long wagon rides over rough and rocky roads, long carries with heavily laden pack baskets and camping accessories, primitive log rafts and open bark camps. None but true sportsmen cared to visit the woods, for it was only the lover of nature who could find sufficient reward to compensate him for the deprivations and hardships incident to a wilderness trip.*

Hotels After the Civil War, however, the region underwent a boom in tourism. Public curiosity was aroused by magazine articles and books like William H. H. Murray's *Adventures in the Wilderness* (1869). Seneca Ray Stoddard's annual guidebooks were especially useful in allaying the fears of city-bred travellers, some of them now moving in family groups. By 1890 the Adirondacks had become a fashionable resort. Dozens of hotels were constructed, from log houses accommodating a few guests to luxurious edifices like the six-story Prospect House, the world's first hotel to equip each of its 300 bedrooms with an electric light.

Camps Guests at these hotels often purchased lakefront lots or a vacation home, which could be anything from a shanty to a dozen cottages requiring a staff of twenty. Many summer cottages today probably date from the boom construction years, between 1885 and 1925.

Private Preserves Along with the growth of camps and hotels was the formation of private preserves. W. E. Wolcott blamed these preserves—there were more than fifty at the time—for the loss of the "perfect freedom" with which the sportsman once roamed the Adirondacks. Writing in 1897, he observed that

> *...at the present time the percentage of people who spend their vacations in bark shanties is very small.*

A. F. Tait, *Still Hunting on First Snow: A Second Shot,* 1855

The purchase of tracts for club-like enjoyment of men in business, the professions, and public life originated with the Lake Piseco Club, which was founded by "gentlemen" from Troy, Schenectady, New York City, Boston and Philadelphia, in 1842. Occupying a log cabin built in 1834, members caught 6,356 pounds of trout in the club's first nine years.

Another club was the North Woods Walton Club, formed in Utica in 1857. Annual forays in the territory between Old Forge and Big Moose Lake, in the western Adirondacks, proved so favorable that several members banded together to buy land. The Bisby Club, established in 1878, became the first association to own a private preserve in the Adirondacks. In such ways was the male monopoly broken by the claims of wives, children and parents to *their* share of the Adirondacks.

45

No generalizations can be made about the many clubs and preserves in the Adirondacks; most were formed during the period 1875–1925 and still retain their early character. The Adirondack League Club is the largest and probably the most luxurious of these, with its 99,000 acres of land, scientific logging of its forests, and its numerous year-round cottages and spacious lodges for members and guests. The Putnam Camp in Keene Valley is far smaller, but it retains much of the atmosphere it had when its members and guests came largely from Harvard University and nearby Boston. William James and Sigmund Freud were just two of the luminaries who stayed at the camp.

Women Women journeyed through the Adirondacks before the Civil War, though the arduous trip, according to accounts in periodicals and journals, was usually made by men and college boys in parties of two to six. Lady Amelia Murray recorded her trip from the Saranac Lakes to Raquette Lake in a book published in her native England in 1856. Accompanied by another woman and two men, plus two guides, she slept on hemlock boughs and an "air cushion" in improvised shelters. A scarlet shawl suspended from the roof discreetly separated the two women on one side from the two men on the other.

The women at Camp Stott frequently fished on Raquette Lake and nearby lakes and streams. In 1895, Mrs. Frank Stott wrote in her diary, "On Friday went to Sumner outlet, a two mile tramp, fished for brook trout and in 4-1/2 hours caught ninety-five." Ann Morgan, daughter of J. Pierpont Morgan, was expert with rod and rifle, as was Pauline Brandreth, who lived year-round for a period of time at her camp at Brandreth Park, a feat much admired by woodsmen but less so by her family. Pauline used the name "Paul Brandreth" for articles she wrote for outdoor magazines.

Enter- An easier-to-reach and more comfortable wilderness did not
tainments lessen a family's enjoyment of the Adirondacks. Photographs indicate that recreation was leisurely and very much a family affair. Sewing, letter writing and reading were activities for the porch; singing accompanied by a piano and perhaps one or two other instruments, such as guitar or mandolin, took place indoors in the evening or on rainy days. Walks in the woods, picnics, boating on the lake were among innocent outdoor diversions. Strenuous exercise, to gather from the evidence, was not common until this century.

Girls' camp at Moss Lake

Two developments in the 1880's, the formation of children's camps and the growth of winter sports, contributed to the ways in which people enjoyed the Adirondacks. Camp Dudley, formed under YMCA auspices in 1885, moved to its present location on Lake Champlain in 1891; it has the longest record of continuous operation of any youth camp in the United States. The regimen which children's camps introduced to summer life is suggested by what a Dudley camper needed to do to win a "Big D" letter in 1905:

1. Swim 50 yards.
2. Win a place in an athletic contest.
3. Row to the Vermont shore and back.
4. Climb a mountain and sleep out one night.
5. Make a shelter and fireplace, and cook a simple camp meal.
6. Do something worthwhile.
7. Contribute to the equipment of camp.
8. Catch and tame a chipmunk, take a picture of a wild animal, or identify 20 birds and 20 trees.
9. Sing a song, tell a story or dance a jig.
10. Earn approval of camp leaders.

Hiker, trail erosion diorama

By 1941 there were 723 youth camps in New York State. The most popular sporting activities were baseball, swimming, boating, hiking and camping, with dramatics, woodwork and nature instruction topping the list of "educational" camp activities. Our idea of the vacation as a time of rigorous, planned and even competitive sport, owes something to these camps and the generations of "alums" they have produced in the course of a century.

The "Wilderness Cure"

Organized camping taught Americans how to enjoy the summer months to the fullest, but it was the health business that grew up around the treatment of tuberculosis in Saranac Lake that contributed to the development of winter sport in the region. Dr. Edward Livingston Trudeau, who contracted the dreaded disease about 1868 but recovered following two prolonged visits to the area near Saranac Lake, opened his Trudeau Sanitarium in 1885. From then until 1948, when the drug streptomycin was discovered, Saranac Lake was the most famous center for the treatment and study of tuberculosis in the United States. In 1929 Trudeau's pioneering sanitarium had a capacity of 160 and had treated some 6,500 patients. Similar institutions were established in the vicinity, so that the Adirondacks were better known to the world as a health resort than a place for vacationing.

A variety of wintertime activities were developed to expose "lungers," as they were called ("consumptive" was taboo), to fresh air and sunshine—as much as a patient's condition would allow. Those still feverish spent countless hours on porches, sitting in recliners by day and sleeping in beds by night, even when temperatures fell below zero. Patients without fever could indulge in mild exercise, such as sleigh rides and winter picnics. One convalescent had his doctors prescribe a stay in the Adirondacks with the following verses:

But the clear-aired North will cure you. Pack
  up your kit and go.
The cold will be your doctor, and your nurse
  will be the snow.

Winter Sport

With upwards of forty percent of Saranac Lake's 1907 population of about 2,000 being patients, all in various states of physical condition and compelled to rest and recover for periods of a year or more, it is no wonder that Saranac Lake became an innovator in winter recreational sport. The Winter Carnival, dating to 1898, is still an occasion for parades and competitive sports on ice and snow. A giant Ice Palace, illuminated from within at night, is the town's annual salute to winter.

Winter Olympics

By 1930 winter sport had evolved beyond being a diversion for the ill. An auto travel guide that year called attention to the town's ski trails and ski jumps, to winter picnics by horseback, ice fishing, hockey, trap shooting, snowshoeing, skating, tobogganing and rabbit hunting. The Winter Olympics in neighboring Lake Placid, in 1932 and again in 1980, represented the crowning of this region of the Adirondacks as a national center of competitive and recreational sport.

49

Adirondack Cottage, interior

were overlaid with sheets of bark, usually white birch, or with
short lengths of split twigs arranged in a variety of geometric
patterns. Chairs of cedar and yellow birch, the bark still on, were
also made. Some rustic furniture was produced for sale, but most
of it seems to have been intended for particular camps, suggesting
that caretakers or employees did this work for the camp owner.
The best rustic work dates from between 1875 and 1925.

Adirondackers worked at expressions besides those done by *Story*
hand. Tales and music were elevated to an art in the Adirondacks. *Telling*
Tellers and singers have mostly vanished, but the tales and tunes
of some have been preserved by tape recordings and by historians
and musicians of folk life. The lumber camp was the setting for
many stories, some tall, some based on personal experience, and
all a mixture of fiction and fact. Others sprang from an occupation
familiar to all Adirondackers: hunting.

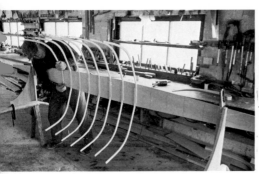

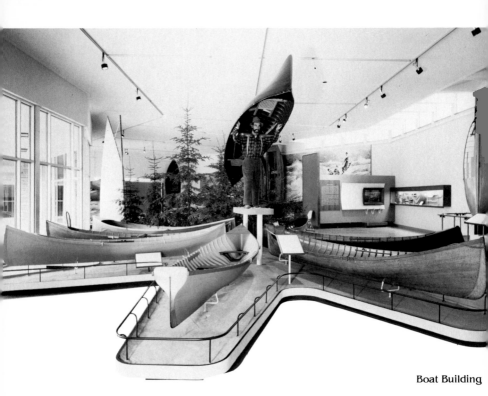

Boat Building

Ham Ferry told the following yarn to folklorist Robert Bethke at Ham's Inn in Childwold in the 1970's:

This Mart Moody from Tupper Lake was another one of them guys. He said, 'I went out one day and here was a big flock of ducks out on Tupper Lake. And I had this good dog. And I shot. And I sent the dog out there. She was heavy with pups, and I didn't know whether I should send her out there. It was a cold day in the fall. Well, she took right off and away she went. And it got dark and she never showed up. And I got to worrying about her. I worried about that dog. She was a good dog, a real good retriever. She'd get anything I'd shot at. So the next morning I woke up and I thought I'd go see if I could find her. And I got down to the shore of the lake and I looked out. And I see something coming. And this dog, she come into shore. She had three ducks in her mouth. And behind her she had seven pups. And each one of the pups had a duck in his mouth.'

Mart Moody was a celebrated guide and storyteller who died in 1910, and Ham Ferry was doing what generations of Adirondack natives have done—entertain by passing along good stories over a cup of coffee or glass of beer.

TRANSPORT AND TRAVEL

Marion River Carry locomotive

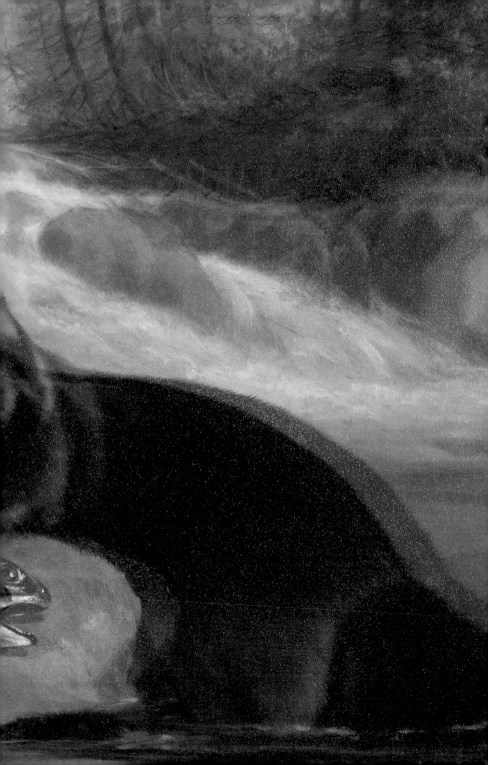

THE IMAGE MAKERS

Camp Cedars by Margaret Bourke-White, 1933

The Adirondacks have always had an image problem, not bad so much as incomplete. The region was described in 1792 as "waste and unappropriated." It was not until the 1830's that the Adirondacks were named, and it was realized that New York's highest mountains were not in the Catskills, but were to be found in the Adirondacks instead. The first comprehensive survey of the Adirondack terrain was conducted by the state not much more than a century ago.

If the Adirondacks, which William Verner, former Adirondack Museum curator, described as "a huge wilderness island poking impudently above the highly civilized sea of the northeast," were perceived by many Victorians as unknown and therefore hostile, for others their appeal lay precisely in the fact that the forests, lakes and mountains were unexplored. It is not surprising, then, that artists and writers have been the chief means by which the general public has been introduced to the Adirondacks and enticed to discover their attractions for itself.

The first to systematically penetrate New York's northern wilderness were parties of scientists and engineers assigned to map and observe the new frontier. They were accompanied by artists and, later, photographers whose pictures at once aroused public curiosity. Portrait painter Charles Ingham was a member of the team that conducted the first State Geological Survey, led by Ebenezer Emmons, in 1837. Ingham's sketches of the journey to the high peaks area appeared as illustrations in the expedition's report of 1838, and his large painting, "The Great Adirondack Pass," was displayed in New York City in 1839. The painting, in which two figures, an artist and man chopping a tree, are dwarfed by the sheer rock face of Indian Pass, is one of the earliest scenes in oil of an Adirondack locale.

The Emmons Report and Ingham's sketches of flora, fauna and the mountainous terrain initially served a practical purpose. Other artists, realizing its aesthetic possibilities, came to the area to sketch from nature what they saw, or thought they saw, in "plein-air," a practice which prevails to this day.

Another early artist was the painter Thomas Cole whose romantic and subjective landscapes, gnarled trees, looming mountains, sweeping vistas and storms, were intended to arouse feelings of awe and mystery. In his depiction of the territory around Schroon Lake, which he visited with Asher B. Durand in 1837, tamed and

Thomas Cole

wild nature confront one another. The painting combines observed fact with fancy; the pastoral foreground with farmhouse and mill is convincing, but the distant mountains, presumably the "high peaks" which Ingham had climbed earlier, resemble the Alps more than the Adirondacks.

Hudson River School Frenchman Régis Gignoux also journeyed to the Adirondacks and imbued his paintings with similar grandeur and mystery. A more frequent visitor was Durand, a friend of Cole's and, with him, a founder of the Hudson River School of painting. Durand made trips to the Adirondacks until 1877, drawing and occasionally painting studies from nature in localities around Lake George, Keene Valley and Elizabethtown. Although Durand's landscapes seem romantic in retrospect, they show an objectivity that Cole lacked, wherein the actual landscape, not an ideal one, determined the design.

Durand was often joined by other artists, among them John Casilear and John Kensett. Considered second generation Hudson River School painters, their paintings were more realistic. Along with Sanford R. Gifford, James McDougal Hart and his brother William Hart, who also painted in the Adirondacks, they were concerned with natural light and atmosphere. Scenes from nature were represented directly and there was little attempt to "improve" on nature. Human figures appeared in their landscapes, but they (like the viewer of the painting) were witnesses and were correspondingly small in comparison with the grandeur of the world before them.

A. F. Tait The artist who did as much as anyone to popularize the Adirondacks was Arthur Fitzwilliam Tait, an Englishman who began making perennial trips to the region soon after he settled in New York City, at the age of 30, in 1850. An avid sportsman as well as an artist, Tait painted scenes of men in pursuit of deer and other quarry in their natural habitat. Tait's depiction of the Adirondacks served as a backdrop for his celebrations of life in the outdoors, conveying not so much a sense of wonder as praise for the recreational possibilities of the Adirondacks as a sportsman's paradise. The vivid realism and action in his paintings set him apart from most of his colleagues, and these qualities found ready buyers for his canvases in New York City. He sold some paintings to the firm of Currier & Ives, which then reproduced them by the hundreds as lithographs for Americans who wanted inexpensive pictures for their homes.

Frederic Remington,
Hunter's Cabin, Silver Lake

Later Painters By the time of the Civil War and the attendant burst of scientific and technological knowledge, romantic ideas about the wilderness were rapidly fading. Photographs began to replace representational landscapes, and the Adirondacks were seen less as a place of mystery and more as a source of pleasure and recreation. Artists such as Homer Martin, Winslow Homer, and Frederic Remington, all of whom painted in the Adirondacks, interpreted their surroundings in their own, personal ways. The Adirondacks had not lost their lure for painters, however, as is shown by a compilation of the names of 425 artists known to have worked in the region before World War I.

By the 1920's the landscape genre had declined and modern styles of art—impressionism and expressionistic—were on the rise. Fewer major painters were attracted to the Adirondacks. John Marin and James Rosenberg both worked here in their own particular idioms. Their subjective evocations of nature would hardly have been recognizable to earlier artists, whose rendering of topographical features had allowed the viewer to identify specific locales. Rockwell Kent was a more recent carrier of the representational landscape tradition of painting in the Adirondacks.

Photographers Photography was partly responsible for the decline of landscape painting. Views of scenery, along with life in hotels and camps, were staple subjects for the growing numbers of professional photographers who brought their cameras to the Adirondacks after 1870. Thousands of their pictures were sold as postcards, souvenirs and illustrations in guidebooks and other publications aimed at luring vacationers to the region.

Seneca Ray Stoddard was the most prolific and most important of early photographers in the Adirondacks. Operating from his studio-home in Glens Falls, he began his picture-taking trips in 1870 and continued doing so for another forty or so years. His photographs, estimated at ten thousand, together with descriptive guidebooks which he published each year, reassured the public that a holiday in the Adirondacks would be a convenient and safe experience.

Amateurs and Professionals Inventions like George Eastman's Kodak camera created a whole new recreational activity in the Adirondacks beginning in the 1880's. Eager to take home a personal record of their travels, Adirondack vacationers heeded Eastman's advice: "You press the button, we do the rest." Successive inventions like the 35mm and the instant camera make amateur photography today more sophisticated and also simpler for those who wish to preserve a piece of the landscape as a souvenir of their visit. Professionals seek out the Adirondacks for artistic and commercial reasons. Eliot Porter took two hundred color photographs over a two-year period for the best-selling book *Forever Wild,* commissioned by the Adirondack Museum in the 1960's. And publishers of *National Geographic, American Heritage* and *Adirondack Life,* among others, regularly carry handsome photographs of the region in their magazines and books.

The visual and natural purity of the Adirondacks has been taken pretty much as an ordained fact of life. Laws and blue ribbon commissions since the period of abuse in the 19th century have asserted that the Adirondacks shall remain unspoiled—"forever wild" is the key term inserted in the Constitution of 1894. Imagine, then, the consternation of residents and friends of the Adirondacks when word began spreading, only as recently as the late 1970's, that acid precipitation was the single greatest threat to the Adirondack environment—its lakes, some of its wildlife, and perhaps even its lush green cover—and that remedies were almost entirely outside the control of New Yorkers. Pollution had become a national problem; indeed, it involved Canada and therefore did not respect international boundaries. Perhaps for the first time, Adirondackers found themselves part of a global issue with real consequences for their own backyard. The Blue Line separating the Adirondack Park from the rest of the world was a barrier no longer, and the problem of image remained unsolved.

A Cozy Nook in West Bay,
1884, Edward Bierstadt

MUSEUM
OF THE
ADIRONDACKS

Log Hotel, 1876

In late 1947 a conversation took place between William Wessels, who operated a summer hotel, the Blue Mountain House, and Harold K. Hochschild who, like others in his family, had been coming to Blue Mountain Lake since 1904. Both were interested in history. One subject discussed, according to a letter written by Mr. Hochschild to a third party, was the need to protect the locomotive and two cars that stood abandoned on the Marion River Carry between Utowana and Raquette Lakes. Another was the "establishment of an historical museum in the Blue Mountain district." A year later the Adirondack Historical Association was formed with Wessels as its president. But it was not until 1953, when the Blue Mountain House was purchased as the site for a museum, that the idea for a museum ceased being a dream. On August 3, 1957, after 36 months in which old frame buildings were torn down, new buildings for exhibits erected and forays made into the Adirondacks to collect wagons, boats and other remnants of the region's heritage, the Adirondack Museum opened its doors to the public for the first time. By the end of the 1983 season, 26 years later, more than 1.7 million visitors had been admitted.

If the conversation is the earliest documented record of the genesis of the museum, it was publication, in 1952, of Mr. Hochschild's book, *Township 34,* a history focusing on Hamilton County, which gave urgency to the establishment of a museum. It would draw on events, personalities and artifacts illustrated by Hochschild in his book, on which he had been working, as his time as chief executive of a large corporation permitted, since the 1920's. The locomotive and cars were moved to the site of the museum and restored, along with such objects as the steamboat *Osprey,* guideboats, stagecoaches, logging equipment, wagons and other horsedrawn vehicles, many of which were pictured in Hochschild's award-winning history.

In the course of time, additional buildings and wings were constructed to hold these growing collections: a painting gallery and Boat Building in 1965 and the Road and Rail Transportation Building, some 45,000 square feet in extent, in 1969, when Governor Nelson Rockefeller was among those dedicating the new facility. Today the museum has 20 exhibit buildings, the latest being the Mining Building which opened in 1983, plus a dozen others besides—all dedicated to the task of telling the history of

Lobby of Log Hotel

the Adirondacks, its people and their relationship to the majestic Adirondack environment. The museum compound consists of perhaps 30 acres, with another 150 or so being a protective buffer around it.

Like almost everything else in the Adirondacks, the museum follows a seasonal rhythm dictated by climate and the ebb and flow of tourists. Except for its first year and a period when it admitted visitors for ten days during the Winter Olympics, in 1980, the Adirondack Museum has always opened on "Community Day," on June 14, and closed its doors on October 15. The spotless condition for which the museum has been praised is due to the clean-up by seasonal staff that starts in early May. For two weeks after it closes the museum is "put to bed" for another long winter. Shelters over the locomotive and the boats on the pond are enclosed to keep them free of ice and blowing snow, plywood sheets are placed in the windows of the Log Hotel, flowering shrubs are covered, water in the pond and the bubble is drained, and snowblowers replace lawn mowers on two Deere tractors. The mallard and wood ducks are returned to a wild fowl farm near Albany, and the brook trout are placed in a local pond or lake.

By November 1 the staff is back to its year-round complement of fifteen. There may be one or two people at work on a special project or two—a craftsman restoring a large boat or an assistant sorting cartons of papers for the librarian. Skeptics notwithstanding, the museum's closed period is not a time of relaxation; for the maintenance crew it is a time to monitor a complex plant (the museum has a dozen furnaces and consumed 45,006 gallons of fuel oil in 1982). For professional and business staff it is a time for putting plans, some conceived one or two years earlier, into execution. Plans usually mean exhibitions, for which the museum has earned an enviable reputation that extends beyond the boundaries of the Adirondack Park and of New York State. Behind each major installation is an investment of not less than one year. The exhibition "Mining in the Adirondacks" took two years of research and collecting, plus a third year, 1982–83, in which to construct a building and design and install the exhibit itself. Consultants are usually engaged to advise and assist with complicated or otherwise specialized projects, but responsibility for conception and execution rests with the museum's professional staff.

The museum offers many services. School children may visit the museum in classes regardless of the season, though distances and travel budgets make these trips fewer than the museum wants. The library is used by about one hundred researchers every year, not counting museum staffers. Among these are professional writers, graduate students and even employees of the state or wood products corporations wishing to examine the library's old maps. Containing about 7,000 books and many more manuscripts and printed ephemera, such as hotel brochures and railroad timetables, the library is the most extensive and important collection of "Adirondackana" anywhere. The museum loans its paintings and artifacts to qualified museums, and, in addition, its collection of historic photographs, now in excess of 60,000 pictures, is consulted by writers and editors for publication in books

On board the locomotive

63

and magazines of every description. The museum itself is a publisher; it has issued about thirty-five books, monographs and catalogues in less than a quarter of a century.

Attendance in the early eighties has averaged eighty thousand each year, not as good as the pre-oil embargo and pre-inflation numbers which exceeded ninety-one thousand three years in succession, in 1976–78, but still respectable given the fact that these figures are generated in one-third of any given year, during the time the museum is open to the public.

The Adirondack Museum has received grants from state and federal agencies that fund museums, but it has been built and operated almost entirely through contributions from private sources. The Adirondack Museum receives less than three percent of an annual operating budget from government funds, a fact mentioned here because surveys of museum visitors reveal that many believe it is supported entirely by New York State. The museum is private and non-profit, and it is chartered by the Regents of the University of the State of New York and accredited by the American Association of Museums.

If nature has always been the measure of the Adirondacks, the story of man in these mountains has been the measure of the Adirondack Museum. Here are the objects he made for work and play, from the crude, horse drawn snow roller to the sculptured guideboat. Here, preserved for generations to see and enjoy, is the beauty he created in response to the beauty around him.

Visitors at the Adirondack Museum, 1983